The Marathon Man

Written by Mary-Anne Creasy

Illustrated by Pat Reynolds

Flying Start
to Literacy®

Contents

Preface

The longest race in the Olympic Games is the marathon. It is a race of more than 42 kilometres. This race is named after a place called Marathon in Greece, where a famous battle happened.

Athens and Sparta were two very powerful cities in Greece. Each city had its own army.

This is the story of what may have happened thousands of years ago when a famous battle took place.

Greece

Marathon

Athens

Sparta

Chapter 1
The enemy is near

"Enemy ships are coming," shouted the small boy as he ran into Phillip's house at Marathon. "They are near the coast and will soon land."

"There will be thousands of soldiers on those ships," said Phillip.

"The army from Athens is in Marathon, but it is not big enough to fight so many soldiers," said Phillip's father. "We need more soldiers to help us, or we will lose the battle. We will be killed or become slaves."

"The king of Sparta has a large army with many soldiers. He is our friend and he will help us. We have to get a message to him," said Phillip.

"But Sparta is nearly two hundred kilometres away. The road is too rocky for anyone on a horse. How will we get a message to them?" said Phillip's father.

"I have been training and I can run for a very long way," said Phillip. "I will run all the way to Sparta with a message for the army. I will go at once!"

Chapter 2
The long run

Phillip ran out of town and up into the hills.

The sun was blazing and it was very hot. The path was narrow and rocky. It became steeper and steeper. Phillip had to be careful not to trip on the rocky path and break his leg.

The sun went down but Phillip kept running. He was very tired. It was getting harder and harder to keep running, but he did not stop.

He had to get to Sparta to get help.

Phillip ran and ran for two days
and two nights. As the sun came
up on the third day he could see
Sparta in the distance.

But Phillip was exhausted. He could not take another step. He tripped and fell.

"What are you doing so far from home?" he heard someone say. Phillip lifted his tired head and saw a captain from the army of Sparta.

Phillip told the captain about the enemy army that was about to attack Marathon.

The captain listened to Phillip. "We will help you to fight the enemy," he said. "But our army will need three days to get ready."

"You will be too late to help us," said Phillip sadly.

There was only one thing that Phillip could do – he had to run straight back to Marathon to warn the army that Sparta could not help them.

After Phillip rested for a little while, he started on the long journey back home.

He ran for another two days and two nights and finally he reached Marathon.

"Phillip, what news do you have?" asked the captain of the army from Athens.

"Sparta cannot help us. They cannot send their army for another three days," said Phillip.

Chapter 3
The battle of Marathon

By now the enemy boats had landed. They had twice as many soldiers as the army from Athens.

The Athenian army could not possibly win this battle. But if they did not fight, they would all be killed. Their families would become slaves. They had to fight for their own lives and for their families.

With a great shout, they ran at the enemy soldiers.

The enemy soldiers rode large and powerful horses.

But the Athenian soldiers had strong spears and were very fast runners.

The Athenian soldiers moved swiftly
between the horses. They fought
fiercely and well because they were
fighting to protect themselves and
their families.

By the end of the day the enemy was defeated. The enemy soldiers fled back to their ships and sailed away from Marathon.

The soldiers from the Athenian army were exhausted. They had been fighting all day.

But they knew that the enemy ships would now be sailing to the city of Athens. They must march more than 42 kilometres from Marathon to Athens and they must leave at once.

Chapter 4
The victory run

News had to be sent to Athens quickly. The people needed to be told that the enemy had been defeated at Marathon. And they had to be warned that the enemy ships were coming to Athens.

The soldiers looked at Phillip.

"I will do it," said Phillip. "I will run to Athens to warn the people."

Phillip ran for three hours over rocky mountains and he did not stop. He arrived at Athens in time to warn the people.

When the enemy ships finally arrived, the enemy soldiers saw that the people of Athens were prepared for battle. The enemy did not attack the city.

Phillip was a hero. His long run from Marathon to Athens became famous.

Phillip was the first Marathon Man.